Published in 2014 by The Rosen Publishing Group, Inc.
29 East 21st Street, New York, NY 10010

Photo Credits: **KEY** tl=top left; tc=top center; tr=top right; cl=center left; c=center; cr=center right; bl=bottom left; bc=bottom center; br=bottom right

CBT = Corbis; DT = Dreamstime; iS = istockphoto.com; SH = Shutterstock; TF = Topfoto

Front Covertr SH; **2–3**tc SH; **4–5**cl SH; **6**cl iS; br SH; **7**bc, br iS; **8**bl DT; cl iS; **8–9**c iS; **9**cr DT; **10–11**cr SH; **11**tr SH; **18**cl TF; **20**cl iS; **20–21**tl SH; **21**cr DT; tr SH; **22**cl, cr DT; br iS; **22–23**tr iS; **23**bc, cl DT; c iS; **24**c, tr CBT; bc, bl, br, tr iS; cr SH; cl TF; **25**tc, tr CBT; bc, bl, br, tc, tl, tr iS; cl SH; c, cr, tl TF; **26–27**tl SH; **27**br iS; **28**cl CBT; bl SH; **28–29**cr TF; **30**cr iS

All illustrations copyright Weldon Owen Pty Ltd

Weldon Owen Pty Ltd
Managing Director: Kay Scarlett
Creative Director: Sue Burk
Publisher: Helen Bateman
Senior Vice President, International Sales: Stuart Laurence
Vice President Sales North America: Ellen Towell
Administration Manager, International Sales: Kristine Ravn

Library of Congress Cataloging-in-Publication Data

Close, Edward.
  Germ warfare / by Edward Close.
    pages cm. — (Discovery education: how it works)
  Includes index.
  ISBN 978-1-4777-6303-2 (library) — ISBN 978-1-4777-6301-8 (pbk.) — ISBN 978-1-4777-6302-5 (6-pack)
  1. Bacteria—Juvenile literature. 2. Viruses—Juvenile literature. I. Title.
  QR57C56 2014
  579.3—dc23
                    2013023587

Manufactured in the United States of America

CPSIA Compliance Information: Batch #W14PK2: For Further Information contact Rosen Publishing, New York, New York at 1-800-237-9932

GERM WARFARE

Edward Close

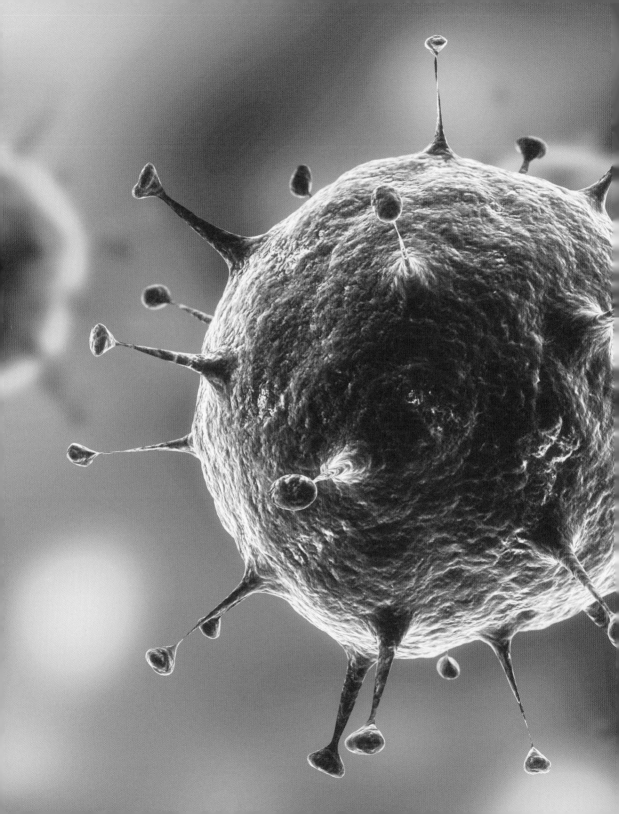

Contents

Discovering Germs

For thousands of years, people wondered how disease spread from person to person. Many believed in the healing powers of gods. It was not until the 1800s that French scientist Louis Pasteur discovered that some microbes, or germs, cause disease. He told doctors about his experiments and discoveries, and advised hospitals to keep their surgery rooms and instruments sterile to prevent the spread of disease.

Early diagnosis
Doctors can now diagnose illnesses much earlier than before. Many people survive diseases today that would have killed them 100 years ago. Regular checkups at your doctor's office will help to keep you and your family healthy.

Covering up
People wore protective face masks during the swine flu outbreak in Asia in 2009. Swine flu is a very infectious disease. A face mask can help limit the amount of airborne germs that a person breathes in.

Under the microscope

In 1674, Dutchman Antoni van Leeuwenhoek built a microscope and became the first person to examine microbes. These days, scientists use microscopes to study microorganisms to find cures for diseases.

HOW TO STOP GERMS SPREADING

When people come in contact with germs, they can become infected with those germs just by touching their eyes, nose, or mouth. Once infected, they get sick. It is usually just a matter of time before the people around them get sick, too. Staying clean and healthy will stop germs spreading.

Regular exercise
If you keep fit and healthy, your body will be stronger and able to fight germs better.

Hand washing
Washing your hands well is the first and simplest way to stop the spread of many illnesses.

Battling Bacteria

You cannot see bacteria, but they are everywhere. There are millions of different bacteria in the world. Less than one percent are harmful and cause illness and disease. The rest are called good bacteria, and they help keep the body healthy, break down food, and recycle waste. Bacteria are also used by scientists to make medicines and vaccines for treating infections and diseases.

Inflammation response
When you cut or scrape your skin, harmful bacteria can easily infect the wound. Your body automatically sends white blood cells to the area to fight infection, and the area becomes red, swollen, and painful as a result.

Signs of bacterial infection
When a bacterial infection occurs, the body produces symptoms. The body temperature may rise, and a wound becomes inflamed. Bacterial infections are common in the throat, stomach, and ears.

Scientists at work

Bacteria can be grown very quickly in the right conditions in laboratories. Scientists use special petri dishes to grow thousands of bacteria, which can then be examined and recorded. Then, the scientists can use the results of their research to better understand how bacteria grow and live.

Under the microscope

Bacteria are so tiny, they are measured in micrometers (1 micrometer = 0.000039 inch). Scientists must use microscopes to examine them. Around the outside of each bacterial cell is a cell wall. Inside is a jelly-like substance known as cytoplasm.

That's Amazing!

Different bacteria have different shapes. They can be round or oval, shaped like a rod, and even a spiral. Many bacteria have thin threads and spikes attached.

Viruses

Colds, chicken pox, and measles are all caused by viruses invading the body. A virus is a minuscule germ that can be seen only under a powerful microscope. It cannot survive for long on its own and must live inside the cells of other living organisms, such as plants and animals. It uses their cells to reproduce itself. Then it spreads, infecting more cells and causing the living organism to get sick.

Microscopic view of a virus

This is what you see when you look at a virus with an electron microscope. This is a powerful microscope that fires electrons at an object and magnifies it by up to 250,000 times. Without electron microscopes, it would be impossible for scientists to study very tiny things such as viruses.

Viral envelope

Spikes that attach to host cell

Helix

Genetic material

Inner coat

Inside a virus
This is a type-A flu virus, which often causes colds and influenza. When a virus invades your cells, the cells are tricked into making more viruses. The cells become damaged or die as the virus spreads through your body.

Signs of a virus
The body produces symptoms to try to overcome a virus. These include coughing, a sore throat, and the headache and high temperature that are part of a fever. This child has viral conjunctivitis, and her symptoms are sore, red, and swollen eyes.

Did You Know?

When you have a cold and your nose runs and you sneeze, those are symptoms that your body is fighting the virus and trying to get rid of it from your nose and throat.

Physical Barriers

B acteria and viruses are all around us. The physical barriers of your body are one way that it defends itself against microbes that can cause infection. Skin, mucus, tears, earwax, stomach acid, and urine are some of the physical barriers to prevent infection. The skin is the first line of defense, keeping most dangerous microbes out, while the airways, bladder, and digestive tract fight infection inside the body.

The human body
Our body is like a machine, with millions of different parts that keep us alive. Adults have 26 billion brain cells, 650 muscles, 206 bones, and many other parts. They all work together so we function properly.

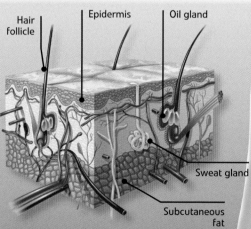

Hair follicle

Epidermis

Oil gland

Sweat gland

Subcutaneous fat

The skin
The skin is the largest and heaviest organ in the human body. It has several layers and acts as a barrier to stop germs invading the body. But if it gets cut or burned, germs may enter and it may become infected.

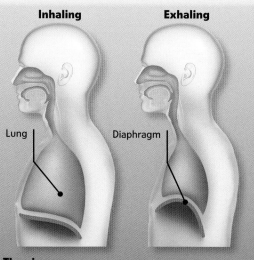

Inhaling **Exhaling**

Lung Diaphragm

The airways
The airways filter out tiny microbes that we breathe in. The walls of the nose, trachea, and lungs are coated with mucus. Microbes in the air become stuck to the mucus, which is coughed up or blown out of the nose.

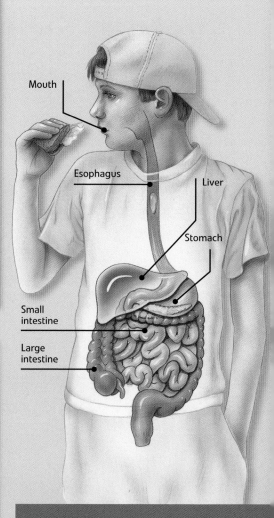

Mouth

Esophagus

Liver

Stomach

Small intestine

Large intestine

Digestive tract
The digestive tract has various barriers to prevent infection. Pancreatic enzymes, stomach acid, and bile break down waste materials while we eat and drink. The intestines contract and shed unwanted cells, helping to remove harmful microbes.

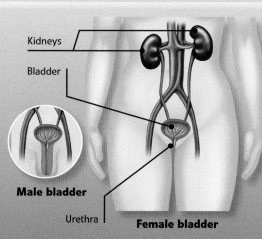

Kidneys

Bladder

Male bladder

Urethra

Female bladder

Urinary system
This system removes waste materials from the body. The kidneys purify the blood. The urethra stops bacteria passing into the bladder. When you urinate, the bladder flushes waste materials from the body, which helps prevent disease.

The Immune System Fights Back

T he immune system is the body's defense against any infectious microbes. It attacks microbes and substances that invade the body and cause disease. It is a network of cells, tissues, and organs, all working together to protect the body and fight infection. It usually does an amazing job of keeping people healthy. But sometimes, problems with the immune system can lead to illness and infection.

Immune response
The immune system produces several substances and agents that attack invading microbes. T cells recognize and kill the invading microbes. Antibodies attach to microbes and either kill them or help other agents to target and kill them.

Macrophage

Bacteria

T cell

B cell

Dividing T cell

Antibody

Macrophage engulfing bacteria

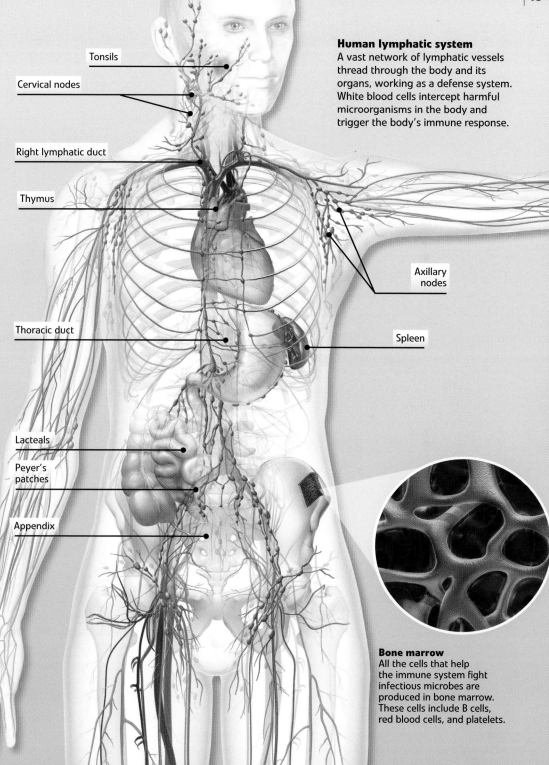

Tonsils

Cervical nodes

Right lymphatic duct

Thymus

Thoracic duct

Lacteals

Peyer's patches

Appendix

Axillary nodes

Spleen

Human lymphatic system
A vast network of lymphatic vessels thread through the body and its organs, working as a defense system. White blood cells intercept harmful microorganisms in the body and trigger the body's immune response.

Bone marrow
All the cells that help the immune system fight infectious microbes are produced in bone marrow. These cells include B cells, red blood cells, and platelets.

The Body's Response

When any body tissue is damaged, the body immediately starts to repair the injured area. If the skin is cut or torn, an inflammation response triggers defensive blood cells and proteins to form a blood clot, which stops the bleeding and blocks microbes. The damaged tissues begin to regenerate and blood vessels slowly produce a blood supply to the cells in the healing wound.

Infection-fighting cells

Inflammation

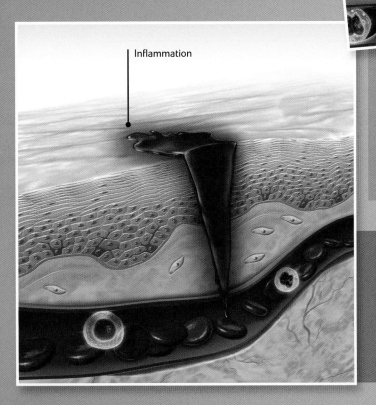

2 Clot formation

A bleeding wound releases a flow of chemicals that attracts infection-fighting cells to the area and triggers formation of a blood clot. This clot is designed to stop the flow of blood from the wound and begin the healing process.

1 Tissue injury

When you cut, tear, or break your skin, there is a risk that infectious microbes will enter via the wound and cause infection and illness. Inflammation, taking the form of swelling and redness, appears around the injured area.

The four key symptoms of inflammation are redness, warmth, swelling, and pain. Changes in blood flow levels to the site are the cause.

Fibroblast

Scab

Granulation tissue

Inflammatory response

An inflammatory response increases blood circulation to the wound site. The blood vessels there dilate and gaps appear in the cell walls so the blood's larger cells can pass through. Increased blood flow means more infection-fighting cells can reach the area, so the immune response is stronger.

Scab falling off

3 Scab formation

As blood vessels take over the wound area, collagen is produced from fibroblasts that migrate to the wound site. The collagen builds up and creates a layer of tissue called granulation tissue. It forms a scab in the process.

4 Healing

New skin tissue develops underneath the scab. Within one to two weeks, the scab falls off. Regenerated, new, pale pink skin can be seen where the wound used to be. Leftover collagen may gradually form a scar.

Our Body's Blood

The cells that make up our immune system are white blood cells, or leukocytes, which are found in the lymph. They grow from stem cells in the bone marrow. There are several types, which work together to seek out and destroy bacteria and viruses. Macrophages consume and destroy germs. Lymphocytes create antibodies, which immobilize the germ so it can be destroyed.

Artery
Arteries have thick, tough, stretchy walls for extra strength.

Blood cell

White blood cell magnified

White blood cells
When invading microbes are detected, white blood cells recognize them and respond. They trigger B cells to produce antibodies, which lock on to the microbes. Antibodies remain in your body, ready for next time.

Blood cell

Outer elastin

Outer layer

Smooth muscle

Inner elastin

Inner lining

Connective tissue

Vein
Thin walls allow a large amount of blood to flow.

Outer layer

Smooth muscle

Inner elastin

Inner lining

Connective tissue

Valve flap

Inside veins and arteries

Arteries carry blood away from the heart. Veins carry blood back to the heart and contain valves, which control blood flow. Smaller blood vessels include capillaries, arterioles, and venules. Their role is to transport blood around the body.

Fever

One way your body responds to injury and infection is with a fever—an increase in temperature. The body's normal temperature is set at about 98.6°F (37°C). But when harmful microbes enter the body, special chemicals tell it to raise its temperature by a degree or two. The higher temperature kills many bacteria and divides the body's infection-fighting cells, which work harder to kill any remaining microbes.

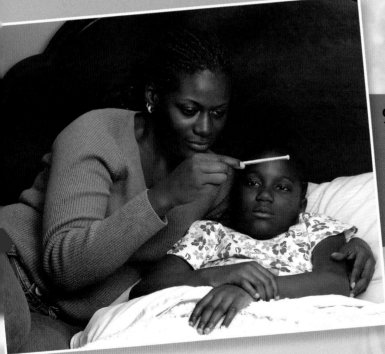

Checking temperature
To diagnose a fever, check your temperature with a thermometer. If it is higher than average for a few days, it is best to be see a doctor. Other symptoms of fever are tiredness, sleeplessness, shivering, and nausea.

YELLOW FEVER

Every year, about 200,000 people contract yellow fever. In extreme cases, people get very tired and sick, their heartbeat slows, and their skin begins to bleed. There is currently no cure for yellow fever and about 30,000 people die from it each year. About 90 percent of all cases occur in Africa.

Mosquitoes
Females spread the disease. They bite an infected person, then bite another person.

Did You Know?

Some diseases, such as malaria, occur only in certain parts of the world. If a sick person has traveled overseas recently, their travel destination may be a clue to the cause of their fever.

Causes of fever

The most common cause of fever is an infection, such as a cold or influenza. Fever sometimes occurs when a person suffers a trauma or injury, or has a bad reaction to antibiotics. Most fevers last fewer than two days and can be treated by your family doctor.

Allergic Responses

An allergy is an overreaction of the body's immune system to harmless substances that it should ignore. Our immune system is designed to fight off invading bacteria and viruses. Sometimes, the body's defenses identify harmless substances such as dust, mold, or pollen as infectious microbes. Immune system cells destroy these harmless microbes, but make us feel sick in the process.

Poisonous plants
Many plants are poisonous or cause severe allergic reactions. Not many will do long-term harm, but it is a good idea to learn which plants may be dangerous so you can avoid them.

Allergic reactions
People can be at risk of getting an allergy because of factors such as their family history, gender, and age. There are also environmental factors such as pollution, exposure to infectious diseases, diet, and the level of allergens.

Bee sting

Injection
Allergic reactions to flying stinging insects, such as bees, hornets, and wasps, are relatively common. Most people develop a reaction at the site of the sting that causes pain, swelling, redness, and itching.

Seafood Peanuts

Ingestion
Some people may suffer an allergic reaction from certain foods. It is common for people to have allergies to nuts, seafood, and dairy products. Their reaction may include vomiting, swelling, a rash, or hives.

Hay fever

With the mild allergy hay fever, the nasal airways swell when an allergic person breathes in pollen or dust. Trying to avoid these things is the best way to prevent hay fever. There are medications that ease symptoms.

Animal fur

Latex

Mold

Pollen

Dust mite

Skin contact

There are many types of itchy skin allergies and rashes. Some people's skin erupts with hives just minutes after contact with an allergen. Certain chemicals, including some found in makeup and hair dye, can be allergens.

Poisonous plants

Inhalation

Breathing in airborne dust, pollen, and mold triggers an allergic reaction in some people. The nose and eyes become swollen and irritated as the body reacts. Sneezing, a runny nose, and itchy eyes are symptoms.

World's Deadliest Diseases

For thousands of years, humans have had to overcome many outbreaks of deadly diseases. Scientists have been able to find cures for some of these diseases, such as bubonic plague and smallpox. However, diseases such as malaria and HIV/AIDS continue to take the lives of millions of people around the world every year. Here are some of the world's deadliest diseases of recorded history.

Bubonic plague
Known as the Black Death, this disease first struck in the 1300s and 1400s, and again in the 1700s. It is estimated it killed nearly a third of the population of Europe, and the worldwide death toll reached 75 million over a 200-year period.

Spanish flu
This outbreak of an influenza strain is believed to be the deadliest in history. Estimates state it killed between 50 and 100 million people worldwide in six months from 1918 to 1919, and that it struck nearly 10 percent of all young adults.

Malaria
Malaria, a mosquito-borne disease, is likely the greatest single killer of humans in all history. Estimates suggest that it kills 2.7 million people a year. It is widespread in tropical and subtropical regions of Africa, Asia, and the Americas.

HIV/AIDS
Acquired immunodeficiency syndrome (AIDS) is a mix of infections resulting from the severe damage to the immune system caused by the human immunodeficiency virus (HIV). Since 1981, it has killed more than 25 million people worldwide.

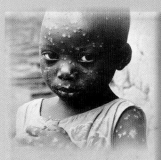

Smallpox
This highly contagious virus affects only humans. It killed at least 60 million Europeans during the eighteenth century, including five monarchs, and about 90 percent of the Native American population in the nineteenth century.

Cholera
This deadly bacterial disease causes extreme diarrhea and vomiting. People are infected mostly by contaminated drinking water. More than 12,000 cholera deaths have occurred since 1991, mainly in very poor areas of Africa.

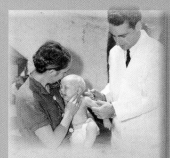

Typhoid
Spread by water and food infected by harmful bacteria, typhoid has largely been eradicated due to better hygiene. An outbreak in the Democratic Republic of Congo in 2004 and 2005 infected 42,000 people, killing more than 200 of them.

Common influenza
The fever, sore throat, aches, and runny nose of the flu are common. But in serious cases, it causes pneumonia, which can be fatal, particularly for very young children and the elderly. In the US, it is responsible for about 36,000 deaths a year.

Polio
This acute viral disease can cause muscle weakness and paralysis, and death in severe cases. Although it has virtually disappeared in the US since a vaccine was invented in 1955, it still occurs in many of the world's developing countries.

Ebola virus
Since 2000, this deadly virus has killed more than 160,000 people in Africa. It has also caused the deaths of many gorillas in central Africa's rain forests. Of the people who contract the disease, between 80 and 90 percent die.

Receiving a vaccination

The most common way to receive a vaccination is by injection with a needle. Scientists have also developed less painful ways of delivering some vaccines. They include nasal sprays, mouth tablets, and even eye drops.

Initial response	Protective immunity	Memory
Antibodies	Weeks	Years
First exposure	Not-obvious reinfections	Mild or not-obvious reinfections

Immune response to vaccination

On the first exposure to the vaccine, the immune response produces proteins called antibodies. Over a matter of weeks, these bind to the disease microbes, eventually killing them. Memory cells are produced and remain for years in the bloodstream, ready to respond to a later infection.

Vaccines and Vaccinations

Louis Pasteur stumbled across a cholera vaccine in his research into bacteria. When he gave chickens a weak dosage of cholera, they no longer developed the disease and became immune. This process is known as vaccination. When a person or animal receives a dead or weakened strain of a disease microbe, the body develops immunity to that disease. The next time the harmful microbes enter the body, it is ready to defend against the infection.

Producing a vaccine
Scientists make a vaccine by isolating a disease microbe and killing it. It still retains its antigen properties and an immune response can be produced. Scientists also weaken a live microbe by changing its growth properties to make a vaccine.

Antibiotics

Antibiotics are drugs that kill bacteria and fungi. Different antibiotics are used to treat different harmful microbes. They were first used in the 1940s, curing many people of diseases that were very common, such as tuberculosis. Over the years, certain bacteria have become resistant to antibiotics, making the treatment of some diseases and infections less successful.

Antibiotics in action
Antibiotics enter the bloodstream and fight off harmful bacteria. Each antibiotic drug is selective and will target and destroy only specific bacteria. But antibiotics cannot kill viruses because viruses are not living things.

Regular medication
It is important to use antibiotics only when it is really necessary. If they are used too often, the bacteria can build up resistance to the antibiotics and make them less effective when fighting an infection.

Alexander Fleming

This British scientist accidentally made an amazing discovery in 1928 when he saw that a green fungus called *Penicillium notatum* had infected a nearby dish of bacteria. The fungus was used to make the first antibiotic, penicillin. Fleming received the Nobel Prize in 1945.

Grow Your Own Bacteria

Bacteria are all around us. They grow in soil, in trash, in water, on plants, and even on us. Thankfully, our immune system usually does a great job of making bacteria harmless and keeping us healthy. Here is how to grow your own bacteria.

What you need:

☑ Petri dish of agar

☑ Cotton swabs

☑ Some old newspaper (to wrap petri dish when disposing)

What to do:

1 Prepare your petri dish of agar, a type of gel used in scientific experiments.

2 To collect a sample of bacteria, rub your cotton swab on a surface in your home that you think may contain germs.

3 Rub the cotton swab over the agar with a few gentle strokes before putting the lid back on and sealing the petri dish tight.

4 Allow the dish to sit in a warm area for 2 or 3 days.

5 Check the growth of the bacteria each day by making an observational drawing and describing changes. What were your results?

6 Try repeating the process with a new petri dish, and collect a sample from under your fingernails or between your toes.

7 Dispose of the bacteria by wrapping up the petri dish in old newspaper and placing it in the trash. Make sure you keep the petri dish lid shut tight at all times.

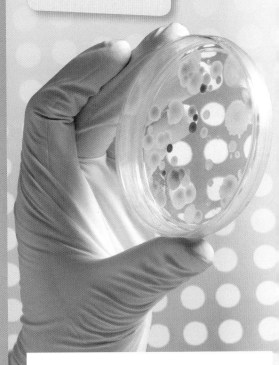

What can we see?

The agar plate and warm conditions are the perfect climate for bacteria to grow. The microbes on the plate will grow into individual colonies, each identical to the original. The bacteria grow steadily, and, after a short time, we can see them in our petri dish. Different samples produce different results. What did your dish look like when you took a sample from your own body?

Glossary

allergy (A-lur-jee)
A reaction our body has when we come into contact with certain allergens, such as pollen.

antibiotics
(an-tee-by-AH-tiks)
Medicines that doctors prescribe to treat infections in our body.

arteries (AR-tuh-reez)
Muscular tubes that carry blood away from the heart to the cells, tissues, and organs of the body.

bacteria (bak-TIR-ee-uh)
Certain types of single-celled organisms without a nucleus.

blood clot (BLUD KLAHT)
A thickened mass of blood.

cell (SEL)
The basic structural and functional unit of all organisms.

immune system
(ih-MYOON SIS-tem)
A system that protects the body from infection and disease.

infection
(in-FEK-shun)
An incident in which a transmissible disease enters our body.

inflammation
(in-fluh-MAY-shun)
A protective reaction of tissue to injury or infection, characterized by pain, redness, and swelling.

influenza
(in-floo-EN-zuh)
Commonly referred to as the flu, this is an infectious disease that can rapidly spread from person to person.

leukocytes
(LOOHK-uh-syts)
Also known as white blood cells, these help the body to fight infections.

macrophage
(MAK-ruh-fayj)
A type of white blood cell that eats bacteria.

microbe (MY-krohb)
An organism so small that it is invisible to the naked eye.

microscope
(MY-kruh-skohp)
A scientific instrument used to see tiny objects such as microbes.

organs (OR-gunz)
Internal, structural parts of our body that have specialized roles.

plague (PLAYG)
Any epidemic disease that has a high rate of death.

tissue
(TIH-shoo)
A part of an organism that is made up of cells with similar structure and function.

vaccine (vak-SEEN)
Medication that helps to prevent us from contracting diseases.

veins (VAYNZ)
Tubes in our body that form a branching system and carry blood to the heart.

virus (VY-rus)
A small, infectious agent that can replicate only inside the cells of other organisms.

Index

Websites

Due to the changing nature of Internet links, PowerKids Press has developed an online list of websites related to the subject of this book. This site is updated regularly. Please use this link to access the list:
www.powerkidslinks.com/disc/germ